Black Widow
SPIDERS

by Eric Ethan

Gareth Stevens Publishing
A WORLD ALMANAC EDUCATION GROUP COMPANY

Please visit our web site at: www.garethstevens.com
For a free color catalog describing Gareth Stevens Publishing's
list of high-quality books and multimedia programs,
call 1-800-542-2595 (USA) or 1-800-387-3178 (Canada).
Gareth Stevens Publishing's fax: (414) 332-3567.

Library of Congress Cataloging-in-Publication Data

Ethan, Eric.
   Black widow spiders / by Eric Ethan.
      p. cm. — (Dangerous spiders—an imagination library series)
   Summary: An introduction to the physical characteristics, behavior, and life cycle of
black widow spiders.
   Includes bibliographical references and index.
   ISBN 0-8368-3765-7 (lib. bdg.)
   1. Black widow spider—Juvenile literature. [1. Black widow spider. 2. Spiders.] I. Title.
QL458.42.T54E84   2003
595.4'4—dc21
                                   2003045557

First published in 2004 by
Gareth Stevens Publishing
A World Almanac Education Group Company
330 West Olive Street, Suite 100
Milwaukee, WI 53212 USA

Text: Eric Ethan
Cover design and page layout: Scott M. Krall
Text editor: Susan Ashley
Series editor: Dorothy L. Gibbs
Picture research: Todtri Book Publishers

Photo credits: Cover © Ron Austing; pp. 5, 7, 9, 11, 17 © James H. Robinson; pp. 13, 19
© A. B. Sheldon; p. 15 © Bill Beatty; p. 21 © James E. Gerholdt

Printed in the United States of America

1 2 3 4 5 6 7 8 9 07 06 05 04 03

**Front cover: The red hourglass shape on
the abdomen of a female black widow
spider signals DANGER!**

TABLE OF CONTENTS

Words that appear in the glossary are printed in **boldface**
type the first time they occur in the text.

BLACK WIDOW SPIDERS

When it comes to black widow spiders, watch out for the females! Female black widows are very dangerous. They are the most poisonous spiders in North America. Their **venom** is fifteen times more poisonous than a rattlesnake's.

The name "black widow" refers to the color of the female spider and to the fact that the females sometimes eat the males. When a female does eat a male, it is usually a mistake. Female black widows have poor eyesight, so males that come to their webs to **mate** are sometimes mistaken for something good to eat.

A male black widow spider is much smaller than a female. Because the males are not known to bite people, they are believed to be harmless.

WHAT THEY LOOK LIKE

Female black widows are shiny and black. Adult females are about 1-1/2 inches (4 centimeters) long, including their legs. Like all spiders, black widows have eight legs, and their bodies are divided into two main parts — the **cephalothorax** and the **abdomen**. The abdomen of a female black widow is large and very round, and it has a red mark on the underside. The red mark is shaped like an hourglass.

Male black widows look very different from females. They are half the size of females, and they are light brown or cream colored, instead of black. Also, males do not have the red hourglass shape on their abdomens.

The red hourglass-shaped mark on this spider's abdomen makes it easy to identify. It is a female black widow!

HOW THEY GROW

While a female black widow might live for up to a year and a half, a male will usually die within a month or two after it is fully grown. During its short life, a male's main job is to mate with females. After mating, the male spider leaves the female's web, and the female prepares to lay her eggs.

A female black widow lays hundreds of eggs at a time. She wraps the eggs in balls of silk called egg sacs. A single egg sac might contain more than a hundred eggs. The spider hangs the egg sacs in her web and guards them until the eggs are ready to hatch.

This female black widow is guarding an egg sac. With more than a hundred eggs inside, the egg sac is almost as large as the spider's body.

Baby black widows, called spiderlings, hatch after about twenty days. When they are born, they are a light color, often yellow, white, or reddish orange. The color becomes darker through a process called **molting**. As a spider's body grows, the hard shell, or **carapace**, that surrounds it does not stretch. During molting, the shell splits open, the spider crawls out, and a new shell forms. A black widow spiderling molts several times. Each time, its color gets darker.

After about three months, black widow spiderlings are fully grown. But of the hundreds of spiderlings that come out of an egg sac, only about one in every twelve reaches adulthood. Insects eat them, and, sometimes, when they cannot find other food, the spiderlings eat each other.

This open egg sac shows how many eggs one sac can contain. The eggs look like small pearls. Some of them have already hatched!

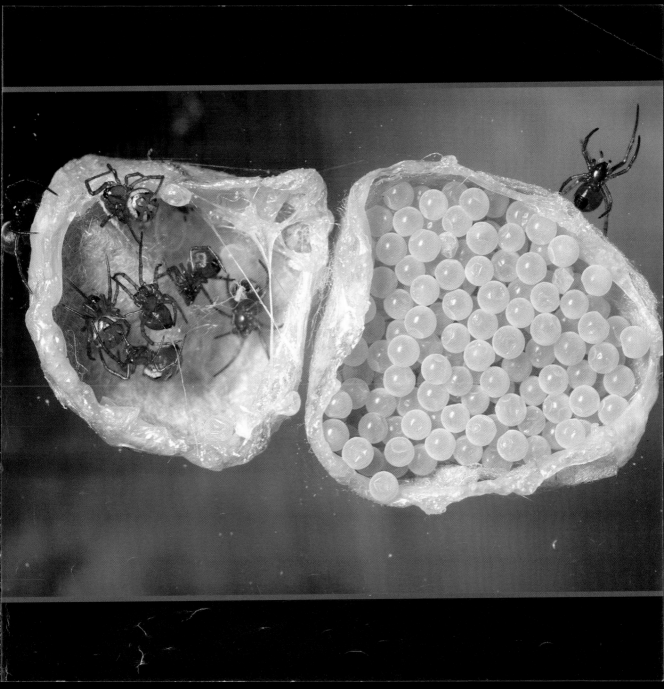

WHERE THEY LIVE

Black widow spiders live in more areas of North America than any other poisonous spider. They can be found in almost every state and as far north as southern Canada. Because these spiders prefer warm climates, they are most common in the southern half of the United States.

Black widows do not like to be disturbed. Their webs are usually close to the ground and in dark, sheltered places, such as under rocks or porches or inside basements or sheds.

The northern widow spider, which also has a red hourglass, is a relative of the black widow. Northern widows live mainly in eastern states.

THEIR WEBS

Like most spiders, black widows spin webs using silk they make in their bodies. The silk comes out of small openings called **spinnerets**. These openings are located at the back of a spider's abdomen. The silk made by a black widow is stronger than the silk of almost any other kind of spider.

There are several different types of spider webs. The type of web a black widow weaves is called a cobweb. Another type is called an orb web. An orb web is round. A cobweb does not have a particular shape or pattern. It looks like a tangled mass of threads. As the black widow spins its web, it uses the comblike hairs on the ends of its back legs to pull and shape the silk.

A black widow starts its cobweb with a single silk thread. The thread comes from a spinneret on the spider's abdomen.

HUNTING FOR FOOD

Black widow spiders do not hunt for food. They hide in their webs and wait for food to come to them. Because they have poor eyesight, these spiders rely on their sensitive legs to tell them when **prey** is near.

When an insect steps onto a black widow's web, the spider's legs feel the vibration. The spider runs to the insect and bites it. Then, to make sure the prey cannot escape from the web, the spider wraps the insect in silk. Biting the prey again, the black widow **injects** it with venom. The poison not only kills the insect but also turns its body tissues into a liquid so the spider can "drink" its meal.

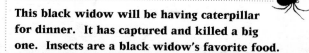

This black widow will be having caterpillar for dinner. It has captured and killed a big one. Insects are a black widow's favorite food.

THEIR BITES

A black widow's bite contains powerful poison. Fortunately, this spider injects only a small amount of poison with each bite. It is enough poison to kill an insect but rarely enough to kill a person. Still, a black widow's bite can be painful and can make a person very sick. The venom attacks the nervous system, which controls a person's muscles and organs, including the heart and the lungs. Anyone bitten by a black widow spider should get medical help right away. A special **antivenin** can fight the spider's poison.

Although female black widows are dangerous, they do not go looking for people to bite. They rarely leave their webs and would bite a person only if they felt threatened or thought their eggs were in danger.

Although this northern widow is closely related to the black widow, its venom is believed to be less dangerous.

THEIR ENEMIES

Because of its poisonous bite, the black widow does not have many enemies. The spider's greatest dangers are mud dauber wasps and humans. When people see a black widow, they usually kill it. Mud dauber wasps, on the other hand, do not kill black widows — at least not right away.

When a mud dauber wasp captures a black widow, it stings the spider to **paralyze** it. The spider is still alive, but it cannot move. Then the wasp takes the spider to its nest and places it in a mud **cell**. The mud cell contains one of the wasp's eggs. When the egg hatches, the helpless spider becomes food for the baby wasp!

Black widows are commonly found around woodpiles. Unfortunately, many people do not see the spider until AFTER it bites.

MORE TO READ AND VIEW

Books (Nonfiction)

Black Widow Spider. *Bug Books* (series). Monica Harris (Heinemann Library)

Black Widow Spiders. *Dangerous Creatures* (series). Bill McAuliffe (Capstone Press)

Black Widow Spiders. *Spider Discovery Library* (series). Louise Martin (Rourke Book Company)

Life Cycle of a Spider. Ron Fridell and Patricia Walsh (Heinemann Library)

Spider. *Killer Creatures* (series). David Jefferis and Tony Allan (Raintree/Steck-Vaughn)

Spiders and Their Web Sites. Margery Facklam (Little Brown)

Spiders Are Not Insects. *Rookie Read-About Science* (series). Allan Fowler (Children's Press)

Spiders Spin Webs. Yvonne Winer (Charlesbridge)

Books (Fiction)

Charlotte's Web. E. B. White (HarperCollins)

Once I Knew a Spider. Jennifer Owings Dewey (Walker & Co.)

The Spider and the Fly. Mary Botham Howitt (Simon & Schuster)

Spider Weaver: A Legend of Kente. Margaret Musgrove and Julia Caims (Scholastic)

Videos (Nonfiction)

Animal Families for Children: The Spider / The Cicada / The Wasp. (Library Video)

Bug City: Spiders & Scorpions. (Schlessinger Media)

Nightmares of Nature: Spider Attack. (National Geographic)

WEB SITES

Web sites change frequently, so one or more of the following recommended sites may no longer be available. To find more information about black widow spiders, you can also use a good search engine, such as **Yahooligans!** [www.yahooligans.com] or **Google** [www.google.com]. Here are some keywords to help you: *black widows, poisonous spiders, spider bites, spiders.*

kidshealth.org/kid/ill_injure/aches/ black_widow.html

"Hey! A Black Widow Spider Bit Me!" is part of the information-packed *KidsHealth* web site. It is the first in a series of pages dedicated to information about a black widow's bite. After learning about the spider, you can click on links to "What a Black Widow Spider Bite Looks and Feels Like" and "What a Doctor Will Do." All of the information has been reviewed by qualified medical doctors.

www.desertusa.com/july97/ du_bwindow.html

This page from the *DesertUSA* web site might be a little harder to read than others, but the information is well organized. Along with descriptions of both adult black widows and spiderlings, topics include behavior, habitat, hunting, and very helpful information about bites. This page also has some good pictures and an interesting table of "Curious Facts."

www.enchantedlearning.com/ paint/subjects/arachnids/spider/ Blackwidowprintout.shtml

Visit this site to learn basic information about black widow spiders and to see a labeled line drawing of a female black widow. The drawing is printable, and you can even "paint" it with an easy-to-use, on-line color palette.

www.bsu.edu/CTT/webquest_examples/ ctt_webquests/CreepyCrawlers/ CreepyCrawlers.htm

The animated spiders on this web site make black widows almost come alive. You will not have the worksheet the site mentions, but you can still do the "hunt for information" activity on plain sheets of paper. The activity is part of a group of "Webquest" projects developed by students at Ball State University. Besides being fun, "Creepy Crawlers" includes Internet links to more great information about black widow spiders.

GLOSSARY

You will find these words on the page or pages listed after each definition.
Reading a word in a sentence can help you understand it even better.

abdomen (AB-doh-men) — the back half of a spider's body, which contains its spinnerets, eggs, heart, lungs, and other organs 2, 6, 14

antivenin (an-tee-VEN-in) — a kind of medicine that helps prevent venom from causing painful wounds, illness, or death 18

carapace (KARE-ah-pace) — the hard shell that covers and protects the soft body of an animal and the organs inside it 10

cell (SEL) — a small hole or open space 20

cephalothorax (sef-ah-loh-THOR-acks) — the front half of a spider's body, to which all eight legs are attached 6

injects (in-JEKTS) — forces a liquid into body tissues through a sharp, pointed, needlelike instrument 16, 18

mate (MAYT) — (v) to join together a male and a female of the same kind of animal for the purpose of producing young 4, 8

molting (MOHL-ting) — shedding a covering, such as skin, on the outside of the body to make way for new growth 10

paralyze (PAIR-ah-lize) — to make unable to move 20

prey (PRAY) — (n) an animal that is killed by another animal for food 16

spinnerets (spin-nuh-RETS) — fingerlike organs at the back of a spider's abdomen, which the spider uses to make silk 14

venom (VEN-um) — poison that an animal produces in its body and passes into a victim by biting or stinging 4, 16, 18

INDEX